·ANIMALS ILLUSTRATED·

Wolverine

This book is dedicated to Grace Niptanatiak, who has
hunted and travelled on the land and raised our family
with just as much passion and love for the animals as our
children. You will live forever in our hearts.

·ANIMALS ILLUSTRATED·
Wolverine

by Allen Niptanatiak • illustrated by Patricia Ann Lewis-MacDougall

INHABIT
MEDIA

Note to Readers: For Inuktut-language resources, including pronunciation assistance for terms found in this book, please visit inhabitmedia.com/inuitnipingit.

Published by Inhabit Media Inc.
www.inhabitmedia.com

Inhabit Media Inc. (Iqaluit) P.O. Box 11125, Iqaluit, Nunavut, X0A 1H0
(Toronto) 191 Eglinton Avenue East, Suite 301, Toronto, Ontario, M4P 1K1

Design and layout copyright © 2021 Inhabit Media Inc.
Text copyright © 2021 by Allen Niptanatiak
Illustrations by Patricia Ann Lewis-MacDougall copyright © 2021 Inhabit Media Inc.

Editors: Neil Christopher and Kelly Ward
Art Directors: Danny Christopher and Astrid Arijanto

We acknowledge the support of the Canada Council for the Arts for our publishing program.

This project was made possible in part by the Government of Canada.

ISBN: 978-1-77227-298-7

Printed in Canada

Library and Archives Canada Cataloguing in Publication

Title: Wolverine / by Allen Niptanatiak ; illustrated by Patricia Ann Lewis-MacDougall.
Names: Niptanatiak, Allen, author. | Lewis-MacDougall, Patricia Ann, illustrator.
Series: Animals illustrated.
Description: Series statement: Animals illustrated
Identifiers: Canadiana 20210176458 | ISBN 9781772272987 (hardcover)
Subjects: LCSH: Wolverine—Juvenile literature.
Classification: LCC QL737.C25 N57 2021 | DDC j599.76/6—dc23

Table of Contents

The Wolverine

The wolverine is part of the weasel family, like skunks, ermines, badgers, and otters. It is the largest weasel that lives on land. Wolverines have a skunk-like appearance, but with a bulky body, short, strong legs, and large claws. The wide neck of a wolverine is very strong and well-muscled. The fur of a wolverine is mostly black with a whiteish ring that runs from one shoulder down to the tail and around the other side of the animal to the other shoulder. This ring of fur can be pure white or brown in colour. Wolverines are known for their musk, a stinky spray that they use to keep other animals away!

Male wolverines usually weigh between 30 and 40 pounds (13 to 18 kilograms), but the biggest males can weigh up to 50 pounds (23 kilograms). Females are a bit smaller, weighing about 20 to 25 pounds (9 to 11 kilograms). Both males and females can get heavier if they have a lot of food, as a wolverine's weight changes depending on how successful they are at finding food.

Adult male wolverines are mostly solitary animals, which means they prefer to live alone, but adult females will sometimes allow their young to live close by for about the first year, until they are of breeding age. Then they will be chased away to find their own territory. Most wolverines live large distances away from other wolverines, except where there is a good food source; then they will be closer together.

Let's learn more about wolverines!

Range

Wolverines live throughout the most northern areas of the globe. In Nunavut, wolverines are usually found in mainland areas, but they are slowly moving northward to the higher Arctic islands, though they are still rare there.

Each wolverine has a home range, an area that it uses for hunting that it will stay in all year round and protect from other wolverines. Male wolverines have a very large range that includes the ranges of a few female wolverines. Female wolverines have smaller ranges. Males protect the females inside their ranges from other male wolverines.

All wolverines mark their ranges with a strong scent, similar to that of a skunk.

Younger male wolverines are often more nomadic, meaning they move from place to place, and are plentiful in areas where caribou migrate south into the wintering grounds, and then northward in the spring to have their babies. It is in these areas that the young, older, or sick caribou are hunted by predators like wolves or bears, which provides a good food source for wolverines to scavenge from.

Skeleton

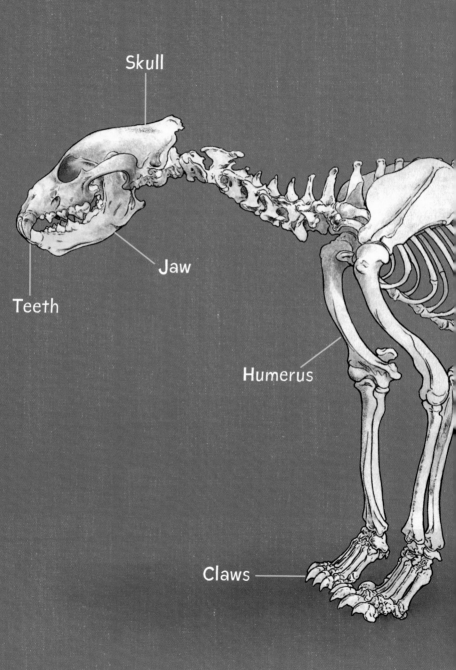

Skull

Jaw

Teeth

Humerus

Claws

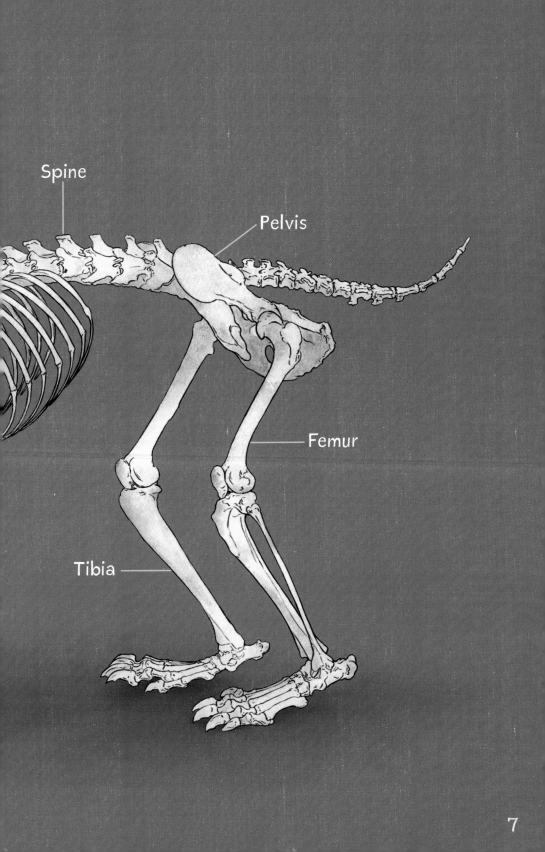

Spine

Pelvis

Femur

Tibia

Diet

Wolverines will eat nearly anything they can find! They are scavengers, which means they feed off the leftovers of animals that have been hunted by other predators, such as wolves or bears. Wolverines have also been observed hunting and have been known to hunt animals much larger than themselves, like muskoxen, moose, and caribou.

Muskox

During the summer months, wolverines usually eat smaller game, such as squirrels, fish, ducks, and young birds. They will also eat eggs and berries. In the wintertime, wolverines eat caribou, muskoxen, moose, deer, foxes, ptarmigans, and rabbits.

Wolverines can also be good seal hunters and will live and hunt on the sea ice when other game cannot be found!

Ptarmigan

Survival Adaptations

Survival in the Arctic can be difficult, and the wolverine has several special adaptations to help it survive.

Wolverines have two types of fur. The outer fur is very long and thick, while the undercoat is shorter and very thick. This helps keep the wolverine warm during the cold winter months.

Fur layers

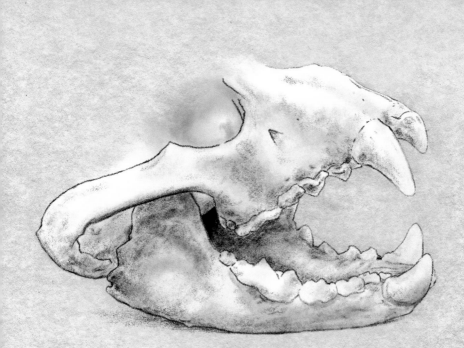

Jaw

Food can also be scarce, and wolverines have adapted to be able to chew and eat the bones of other animals. With their strong jaws they are able to crunch through bones, and—unlike other animals—their stomachs can digest the bones, using them for energy as well as a source of calcium. This helps them survive when other food sources cannot be found.

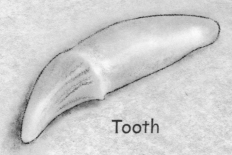

Tooth

Babies

A baby wolverine is called a "kit." Female wolverines give birth to kits in the early spring in a den in the snow that is lined with leaves and grass. They make their dens in places that are safe from predators, like on cliffs, among heavy willow, or in treed areas. Female wolverines usually have 1 to 2 kits. If food is particularly plentiful, 3 to 5 kits may be born.

When kits are born, they are blind and have almost no fur. They are completely white for the first few months of life and will gradually turn black-brown as they get older.

Kits stay with their mothers for some time (sometimes up to two years) as they learn to hunt and survive on their own.

Tough Animals

Wolverines have no predators in the Arctic other than humans. But they do end up in conflict with other animals from time to time. Wolverines are quite good at stealing food and will even steal from wolves and bears when they need to. They have been known to pester grizzly bears until the bear leaves its catch. Wolverines have powerful jaws that can crush the leg bones of caribou and muskoxen, so they would not have a problem breaking the bones of wolves or other predators.

Wolverines have a reputation for being aggressive, but they do not attack human hunters. When a wolverine senses danger, it will usually run away to the safety of rocky hills or cliffs.

Hunting Adaptations

Wolverines are well-built for life in the Arctic, and they have several special adaptations that make them excellent hunters.

Wolverines have very large paws. These large paws work like snowshoes, letting the wolverine walk and hunt much easier in soft snow. Their paws are also very strong, with large claws, allowing them to bury food, build dens, and defend themselves from other animals.

Wolverines are also very strong and muscular. They can carry pieces of meat much heavier than their own body weight. Their short, muscular legs help them carry very heavy food items, which they store in their dens for later. If a wolverine has food to store, it will spray the food with its stinky musk so that other animals will not find it!

Paw

Fun Facts

Wolverines are very good tree climbers! They have been observed very high up in treetops, waiting for danger to pass them by.

Unlike wolves and dogs, wolverines cannot bark or howl. They make growling and grunting noises or loudly snap their jaws to communicate.

Because of their foul-smelling musk, wolverines are sometimes called "skunk bears"!

Traditional Uses

Wolverine parka trim

Wolverine fur is traditionally a valuable and prized fur used as parka trimming or for making mitts. The fur does not wear out as quickly as other furs, and frost does not stick to the fur, so it can be easily brushed off.

In very early times, Inuit ate wolverine meat, but this has not been practised in a long time.

Wolverine mitts

Allen Niptanatiak is a hunter and trapper from Kugluktuk, Nunavut.

Patricia Ann Lewis-MacDougall was born and raised on the Niagara Peninsula. Her childhood days were spent in the woodsy setting of Ontario's Bruce Trail. After graduating high school, Patricia Ann enrolled at Sheridan College to study animatio in the 1980s, and later illustration. She worked for several years as storyboard artist for Nelvana. She has illustrated several books for children.

www.inhabitmedia.com